DISASTER!

FLOODS

By Dennis Brindell Fradin

Consultant:
Robert A. Clark, Ph. D.
Associate Director
NOAA - National Weather Service (Hydrology)

 CHILDRENS PRESS, CHICAGO

In Fort Wayne, Indiana, the St. Marys and St. Joseph rivers meet to form the Maumee. The spring thaw and heavy rains of 1982 caused the three rivers to overflow their banks and flood the town.

For Jill Ann Roth

Library of Congress Cataloging in Publication Data

Fradin, Dennis B.
  Floods.

  (Disaster!)
  Includes index.
  Summary: Explains the causes of one of the most
destructive natural phenomenons, listing some
disastrous floods and explaining protective
measures which should be taken.
    1. Floods—Juvenile literature. [1. Floods]
I. Title. II. Series: Fradin, Dennis B.
Disaster!
GB1399.F7   1982   363.3'493   82-9402
ISBN 0-516-00856-0   AACR2

TABLE OF CONTENTS

The rising water of the Big Thompson River flowed over U.S. Highway 34 (above) and surrounded state patrolman Hugh Purdy. This picture was taken at the mouth of the canyon, looking upstream toward the Narrows.

1/THE BIG THOMPSON RIVER FLASH FLOOD - 1976

On the evening of July 31, 1976, the Big Thompson River in northern Colorado began to flood. "We've got to start taking people out!" Colorado State Patrolman Bob Miller reported by radio. "My car's going to be washed away. . . . I'm up to my doors in water. . . . I'm trying to get out of here before I drown. Got to get to a higher level!"

In spite of its name, the Big Thompson River is normally just a small mountain stream. Its usual depth is about two feet. Its width in most places is usually fifteen feet or less. The Big Thompson isn't one of Colorado's longer rivers, either. It winds for about twenty-five miles inside the Big Thompson Canyon and for about thirty-five miles outside the canyon. To the people who lived alongside the Big Thompson, a major flood of their small river seemed impossible—until the night of July 31, 1976.

In a freak rainstorm that evening, the river grew monstrous. Along the western slopes of the Big Thompson Canyon, more than twelve inches of rain fell. This was a normal year's worth of rain for the region. The river drained water from hundreds of square miles of land. The Big Thompson rose higher and higher.

At 7:35 P.M. the National Weather Service office in Denver issued a warning that "there could be some flooding" in the canyon region. Officials then sent out the state patrol to investigate. Bob Miller was one of those officers. Miller made it safely to higher ground. But another state patrolman, Hugh Purdy, wasn't as lucky. Purdy was surrounded by rising water on U.S. Highway 34, the road that runs inside the canyon.

Cars were pounded and smashed against the canyon walls. Some, like this twisted piece of steel, were battered beyond recognition.

"I'm right in the middle of it, I can't get out!" Purdy radioed. He said something about "high ground," but his words were unclear because of static. Officer Purdy then became one of the flood's first victims when his car was swept off the highway by a torrent of water. Purdy's body was found later, eight miles from where he'd sent that last message. When his car was recovered, it looked like scrap metal from an auto-wrecking yard.

The river began to flow onto the highway in places, and officials knew they had to warn people in the canyon. Approximately three thousand persons were in the canyon that night. Six hundred of them lived year-round in the canyon's small towns. The rest were vacationers who had come there to camp, fish, climb, and enjoy the lovely scenery.

"Get to higher ground! There's a flood!" warned the state patrol and sheriff's deputies. They used the loudspeakers on their cars and even went door-to-door to spread the message. Some people heeded the warning. Others didn't.

Tremendous damage was done to the only road between Loveland and Estes Park. In many places, the river ripped out great chunks of the road (above).

"We've had hard rain before and we got through it," one resident told a police officer. There wasn't enough time to convince the disbelievers. Nor was there enough time to warn all the people. The Big Thompson was undergoing a *flash flood*—a disaster that gives little or no warning.

The Big Thompson Canyon slopes downhill from west to east. By nine o'clock the river was cascading down the canyon like a giant waterfall. The roar of the water and the sight of it overflowing the riverbanks convinced people to leave their homes, trailers, and motels. Some scrambled on foot to higher ground. Many who tried to drive out found that the water was ripping huge chunks right out of the highway. Cars were swept away by the onrushing waters, then pounded and smashed against the canyon walls.

These pictures, taken on the morning of the Big Thompson flood, show Mr. and Mrs. H.L. Huggins at their motel. Mrs. Huggins is standing on a rear balcony that overhung the river. Behind Mr. Huggins is the mountain they climbed to escape the flood. Their car was never found.

"You could hear the people inside the cars screaming for help." said Mrs. Dorothy Venrick, who lived about 250 feet from the river in the town of Drake. "Above the roar of the river and the sound of homes smashing into each other, you could hear the people screaming in their cars. It made your heart sick to stand there and know that there was nothing you could do."

H. L. Huggins and his wife, RoxaBelle, were two of the people who found themselves floating away in an automobile. The couple escaped from their car and climbed up onto higher ground. "Our car just disappeared—we never did find it," Mr. Huggins later said.

As Mr. and Mrs. Huggins climbed to safety, Mr. Huggins turned around and saw a motel floating down the river. "It was the motel where we had been staying," he explained. "I saw people standing on the roof. It didn't go very far and then it disintegrated. The people on the roof were lost—except for one lad who managed to grab onto a tree."

This house was carried downstream and dumped on a bridge just below the town of Drake.

The Big Thompson River reached a height of thirty feet against some of the canyon walls. Water rushing downhill at high speeds—millions of tons of it—picked up and destroyed everything in its path. Concrete bridges were ripped away as if they were toys. Houses, restaurants, and motels were swept off their foundations and then smashed to pieces against the canyon walls. "I could see homes, pieces of homes, trailers, mobile homes, trees, and cars rushing down the river," remembered Dorothy Venrick. "Propane tanks were exploding on and under the water. We could see and hear the explosions."

Dozens were drowned and dozens more were dashed to death against the canyon walls. But there were some amazing survival stories. One woman grabbed hold of a television aerial that was anchored in the ground. The surging water lifted her from the aerial to the roof of her house. She survived the flood by remaining on her roof for four hours. Elsewhere, two emergency medical technicians survived by

Part of this A-frame house floated down the river and was deposited on the bridge at the west mouth of the Narrows.

standing on a cliff ledge all night. A five-month-old boy miraculously survived on top of a rock in the middle of the river.

The flood continued late into the night. Finally, the rain ended. By dawn, the flood was over.

Early that Sunday morning the survivors came down from trees and rooftops. They scrambled down from canyon ledges and came out of their homes. "I can't describe the way the town of Drake looked—I never saw so much death and destruction," remembered Dorothy Venrick, the postmaster of the town. "Everything was covered with water and mud. Trees were uprooted. There were clothes, shoes, and suitcases scattered all over. Cars were buried in the mud— some totally."

That Sunday—August 1, 1976—was supposed to be a happy day in Colorado. It was the one-hundredth birthday of the state. Instead of celebrating, the people faced the worst natural disaster in Colorado's history. One hundred and thirty-nine persons were dead. In the tiny town of Drake, forty of its two hundred residents had perished. Bodies were found inside cars, up in trees, wedged in the canyon rocks, and buried in the mud.

That Sunday morning, helicopters were sent in to rescue those still stranded in the canyon. It was difficult for the National Guard and army pilots to fly the choppers into the narrow canyon. "It was like flying down a tunnel," one pilot said later. In places, the blades of the choppers came to within twenty-five feet of the canyon walls. Yet the pilots successfully completed all of their rescue missions. By evening, about nine hundred persons had been airlifted out of the canyon.

The Red Cross and the Salvation Army came in to help feed, clothe, and house the survivors. Schoolchildren and religious groups helped people clean and rebuild their homes. But little could be done to console those who had so suddenly lost relatives and friends.

The road through the Big Thompson Canyon was wrecked by the river.

*Above: This picture of the Nicholson family in front of
their home was taken the spring before the Big Thompson flood.
Below: After the flood, no trace of the house remained.*

2/SURVIVORS - BIG THOMPSON FLOOD, 1976

Long after their houses and towns were rebuilt, the survivors of the Big Thompson River Flood of 1976 remembered the night the river killed so many of their loved ones. Here are the stories of some of those survivors.

Christine, Howard, and Barbara Nicholson - Loveland, Colorado

"I had my first job that summer—I washed dishes in a restaurant," Christine Nicholson remembered five years after Colorado's worst flood. "It seemed just like any normal day. I rode my bike three miles home from work as usual. It wasn't even raining, and it didn't rain at all until about eight or nine at night. In the evening I took a shower, washed my hair, and came downstairs. Except for the twins, who were sleeping, our whole family was watching TV. I was sitting there combing out my hair when my mom thought she heard something."

"It sounded like the wind," said Christine's mother, Barbara Nicholson. When the family dog began howling, Mrs. Nicholson went outside to investigate.

"While I was outside on the porch, I heard this sound echoing in the canyon," said Mrs. Nicholson. "It sounded like three freight trains off in the distance. I didn't know what it was, but then I saw the water rising on our property. Our house was only about fifty feet from the river. I knew that we had to get our family away from the house and up on the mountain—fast."

The Nicholson family split up into two groups. Mrs. Nicholson took Christine's brother and three sisters up onto higher ground. Fourteen-year-old Christine and her dad stayed in the house for a short while to gather some things.

"Dad went into the garage and got my pet rabbit for me," Christine remembered. "I wanted to go warn neighbors—Mrs. Bailey and her son—about the flood. Dad said that he'd meet me with the car at their house."

Christine rang the Bailey doorbell. Mrs. Bailey's son answered. "Keith, we have to get out of here," Christine told him. "The water is getting high!"

Christine and her dad and Mrs. Bailey and her son headed toward the Nicholson car. Keith Bailey got inside the car. Then Mrs. Bailey remembered some things that she wanted to get out of her house. Christine and her dad went back to help her.

"When we came outside again, the water was all around the house," continued Christine. "The water knocked all of us down. Suddenly we were in the flood—drifting past houses and getting struck by a lot of debris."

"You've got to realize that by the time the flood hit us, it wasn't just water," continued Mr. Nicholson. "There was a lot of solid material—dirt, rocks, buildings, cars, and concrete—that was carried along with us."

Mr. Nicholson and Mrs. Bailey were stopped by a barbed wire fence. It cut them, but kept them from being swept any farther. After untangling themselves, they found they were in calmer water. While heading for higher ground, Howard Nicholson turned around and saw the car, with Keith Bailey in it, floating down the river. That car was found later, seven miles away. Keith Bailey was dead.

Christine saved herself by grabbing a huge cottonwood

*Top left: Barbara, Christine,
and Howard Nicholson
Above: Mrs. Bailey and Howard Nicholson
Left: Christine in 1981, five
years after the flood*

tree. She clung to it for dear life. From the tree, Christine
waded into a neighbor's orchard. "I was by myself now, and I
was really, really scared," she said. "I didn't know where Dad
and Mrs. Bailey were and I was afraid that the water would
come and get me again. I started up the mountain toward the
highway. It was so dark, the only times I could see were when
lightning struck and brightened things up. I got halfway up the
mountain, sat down by a pine tree, and started to cry."

When she finally reached the highway, Christine spotted
her father coming up the hill with Mrs. Bailey. "Go get help!"
her father said. "Mrs. Bailey's hurt really bad."

Christine stopped a police car, and Mrs. Bailey got inside it.
She was later taken to the hospital, where she was treated for
an injured arm and cut hand. Christine and her father got into
a passing pickup truck.

15

After taking the other children to a nearby motel, Mrs. Nicholson had returned to look for her husband and Christine. She spotted them in the pickup. "When we met, we held onto one another and cried," Mrs. Nicholson remembered. "I had been afraid that they'd been lost in the flood."

Christine and her dad and mom joined the rest of the family at the motel. "All night long we could hear huge boulders rolling down the river and colliding," said Mr. Nicholson. "They actually shook the motel. All that night I was confident that our house would be there in the morning. When I went back I could hardly believe it. Where our house had been there was absolutely nothing except the river. The house, the huge trees—even the ground under the trees— were gone. One of our cars was totally buried in silt and mud. The only way anyone knew it was there at all was because a C.B. antenna was sticking out."

"To lose friends and have my home washed away was the worst experience of my life," Christine Nicholson concluded. "I wish we could have gotten some kind of warning. Keith and the others might have survived."

John McMaster and George Woodson - Loveland, Colorado

"When that wall of water hit our ambulance I felt sheer terror," John McMaster recalled five years after the flood. "It was that point in time when you know you're going to die—no ifs, ands, or buts about it."

When the flood struck, John McMaster and George Woodson were in one of the worst possible places. They were in an ambulance inside the steep, narrow portion of the canyon called the Narrows. McMaster, owner of his own ambulance company, was driving the vehicle. Woodson, a schoolteacher working for McMaster during the summer, was in the seat next to him. Both men were emergency medical technicians—people trained to care for others in emergency situations.

Until the flood, McMaster and Woodson had experienced an uneventful day. "It was kind of a dull day, in fact, with not many calls," McMaster remembered. "We had heard on our radio that there was a possibility of a flood. We explained that to the people at the hospital when we brought in a patient.

"Then, that evening, we were told that there was an emergency up at the power plant, so we started heading that way," McMaster continued. "When we got to the river we turned our strong lights on it and lit it up like daytime. The river was nice and low and moving along slowly. It was so peaceful you could have gone out fishing on it."

While traveling along Highway 34, McMaster and Woodson encountered a police roadblock. "They were stopping cars, but they waved us on because we were in an emergency vehicle," George Woodson explained. "When we entered the Narrows we could see the river rising, and we could see things floating in it."

Staring at the propane tanks, trees, and other debris in the river, George Woodson said, "We don't belong here, John!"

"We'll make it through all right," McMaster answered.

McMaster changed his mind when they encountered a large tree blocking their way. He was trying to turn the ambulance around when he heard the roar of the water coming down the canyon.

"There was a huge, choking dust cloud ahead of the water," said McMaster. "Then the water hit us like a big

*John McMaster (top left) and
George Woodson (top right) were
in an ambulance inside the Narrows
(center) when the flood struck.
The ambulance (shown before and after
the flood) was totally destroyed.*

freight train. It picked up our ambulance about fifteen feet into the air and slammed it into a V-shaped wedge on one of the canyon walls.''

McMaster grabbed the microphone and sent one last message: ''We're caught in a flood, we're in the Narrows!''

''John, get out!'' George Woodson yelled, climbing out the window.

''I'm right behind you!'' McMaster answered.

Soon after the two men made it out the window, the water snatched the ambulance out of the canyon wall and sent it smashing against the opposite canyon wall. Parts of the ambulance were later found several miles away.

While their ambulance tumbled downstream, McMaster and Woodson clung to the canyon wall. The Narrows received the highest water of any place along the canyon—about thirty feet. Holding onto ledges and rocks, McMaster and Woodson had to keep climbing to escape the rising water.

''It was pitch black, we couldn't see,'' Woodson explained. ''We just grabbed hold of rocks and climbed up that canyon wall. There was no way we could climb all the way out of the canyon. It was too steep and hundreds of feet high.''

The two finally found a perch about fifty feet above the highway. They were on that ledge for only a few minutes when the rocks John McMaster was holding to and standing on gave way. ''I fell about twenty-five feet straight down, but as I fell I put out my arm and caught a rock,'' McMaster recalled. Although the rock injured his arm, it stopped him just short of the water.

''As I held onto this rock, the water rose higher and higher,'' said McMaster. ''First it was at my ankles, and then it was at my knees, and then it was near my waist. George tore his clothes into strips and made a rope for me to climb, but I couldn't do it because of my injured arm. I was sure I'd drown. Luckily, the water didn't get any higher than my waist.''

For about four hours McMaster held onto the rock on the canyon wall, and Woodson stood on the ledge above him. ''It was pouring rain, and I got extremely wet and cold,'' George Woodson remembered. ''My hands and feet were numb. I kept thinking about my five children. I didn't want them to grow up without their dad, and that helped me hold on.''

At about one in the morning, the water began to recede. By two, water covered only half of the highway beneath them. McMaster and Woodson carefully inched their way down to the highway. Once there, they heard a report on their emergency pocket radio about a burst dam up the river. This report turned out to be false, but McMaster and Woodson didn't know that at the time. They did know that a burst dam could cause more flooding. They climbed back up the canyon wall and spent the rest of the night on a ledge.

''We saw helicopters going over us all night long,'' McMaster said. ''I flashed my cigarette lighter at them, but they didn't attempt to rescue us that night.''

At about seven in the morning, McMaster and Woodson again came down from the canyon wall. At about eight-thirty, a helicopter made the dangerous trip down into the canyon. While the chopper hovered close to the ground, the two men climbed inside it. Then the pilot rose up and over the canyon walls.

Once out of the canyon, McMaster and Woodson were taken by ambulance to the hospital. John McMaster needed stitches in his injured arm. George Woodson was treated for *hypothermia*—a severe loss of body heat. By the next day, both men were back home with their families.

"It took me months to convince myself that I had really gone through that experience and survived," John McMaster said. "For a long time I had trouble sleeping. Every time I'd close my eyes I'd see the water. To this day, if there's a thunderstorm during the night, I wake up with a nightmare."

Clarence Johnson - Drake, Colorado

"I caught hold of some bushes—otherwise I'd have been down the river with the rest of them," eighty-year-old Clarence Johnson remembered five years after the Big Thompson flood. The grandfather of thirteen, Johnson had quite a tale to tell. At the time of the flood, Johnson had known and loved the canyon for over half a century. "I was born in Missouri in 1901, but I came to live in Colorado in 1922. The first Sunday I was in Colorado, I came to see this canyon. The river was so clear that when I got thirsty I lay down and drank right from it.

"In the 1920s fewer people lived in the canyon than now. But then people discovered the great beauty here and built houses and motels inside the canyon. Some were built sticking out over the river. The people wanted to hear the sounds of the water.

"On the night of the flood, our lights went out at about fifteen to nine. Then my wife, Marjorie, and I heard the river making a little extra noise. I went out and walked a little way to the river. It was about two feet higher than usual, which meant that it was only about four feet high. I went back to the house.

"At about that time we heard a voice coming over a loud-speaker on a police car. We couldn't hear what the man was saying because of the noise of the river. It must have been Officer Purdy. He was warning us and the other people to leave. A few minutes later he lost his life.

"I saw some people waving flashlights from some nearby houses. So while a neighbor woman and my wife went up to our shed, which was on higher ground, I took my flashlight and went out onto the front-porch steps. I signalled for the people to come over to our house. I was standing there on my porch steps when the wall of water came. It was just before nine o'clock. The water carried both me and the steps away. Then the porch steps went out from under me, and I went clear under."

Johnson couldn't swim, but that didn't matter. No person could swim in that tremendously strong current. Yet the very speed of the water kept him from sinking completely. Although he swallowed some water, the elderly Johnson was able to keep his head up as he was carried along.

"Later it was figured that the water was traveling about twenty-five miles per hour, but my guess is that it was going much faster than that," Johnson continued. "As I was carried along, I saw that the water could take me in any one of three directions. If the flood carried me to my left, toward the river, there was nothing to stop me from drowning. If I was carried straight, I would run into another house, and I figured that would stop me. If I went to the right, I could try to grab a clump of bushes.

"The water carried me to my right. I grabbed for one clump of bushes, but the bush broke right off in my hand. Then I reached for another bunch of bushes. I grabbed two of them and held onto them tight. It was lucky that I was carried to those bushes. The house that I had hoped to reach was washed away."

22

This picture of Clarence and Marjorie Johnson was taken in July, 1976, just before the flood. Clarence was standing on the front steps (see picture at left) when he was washed away by the rushing river waters.

Holding onto the bushes, Johnson pulled himself out of the water. He then climbed up to the shed where his wife and the neighbor had taken shelter.

"What happened?" Marjorie Johnson asked, looking at her mud-covered husband.

"The river came up and took me downstream!"

His arms and legs were skinned, and he had a bad case of the chills. Otherwise, Johnson was unharmed. Clarence and Marjorie Johnson and their neighbor covered themselves with an old canvas and spent the rest of the night in the shed.

"It was a sorry sight Sunday morning," Johnson continued. "Thirteen houses in our little neighborhood had been washed away, and thirteen people in those houses had lost their lives. We knew all of them. Some were the people I had seen signalling with their flashlights.

"At about eight-thirty in the morning, a copter picked us up and took us out of the canyon. We had to rent a house in Loveland for over a year. Our house had been moved off its foundation and spun sideways."

The floodwaters moved the Johnson house off its foundation and spun it sideways (left). These two hundred-ton rocks dumped in their yard (right) could not be moved.

House movers turned the Johnson home around and placed it back on its foundation. Children from nearby schools helped Mr. and Mrs. Johnson clean up the house. The Army Corps of Engineers came in to move huge boulders and other debris out of the flooded area.

"They used the biggest tractors I ever saw," Johnson recalled. "One rock they moved from in front of our house weighed ten tons, they said. There were three huge rocks a little way from out house that couldn't be moved. An engineer estimated that each weighed a hundred tons.

"I know for a fact that the water carried these huge rocks about four miles, because there was only one place in the canyon that had rocks like that. Human beings can't do anything about it when they're caught by such power. The best thing is to get out of the way of a flood—if you're lucky enough to have a warning."

3/THE CAUSES OF FLOODS

Thousands of years before people built towns, rivers cut channels across the continents. Sometimes the rivers overflowed their banks and flooded. When that happened, the floodwaters spread rich soil throughout the nearby valleys.

The first cities were built about 5,500 years ago. Some of the most important ones grew alongside five rivers: the Indus River in Pakistan; the Nile River in Egypt; the Yellow River in China; and the Euphrates and Tigris rivers in the Middle East. The valleys of these rivers are called the "cradles of civilization" because many of the first cities were built there.

Floods and Ancient People

Early people found many advantages to living near rivers. That rich soil spread by past floods helped farmers grow fine crops. The rivers provided the best transportation that could be had at the time. The rivers also were important in daily life. They provided water for drinking, cooking, bathing, and washing clothes.

There was one bad thing about living near the rivers. Sometimes they flooded up and over their banks. When that happened people were drowned, towns were destroyed, and crops were washed away. After the floodwaters subsided, the people usually returned to rebuild their towns. The good things about living in the river valleys greatly outweighed the bad.

*Deucalion and Pyrrha scattered stones across
the land so the human race would continue.*

"Why do the floods come?" ancient people wondered.
Many thought that floods were punishments sent by the gods.
Almost every group of people who experienced floods told
flood stories as part of their religion or mythology.

According to an ancient Greek story, Zeus, the king of the
gods, looked down from the heavens and saw that people
were wicked. Zeus decided to destroy the human race. He
sent rainstorms to flood the land. Zeus also asked his brother
Neptune, the sea god, to stir up the oceans. Together the two
gods drowned almost all of humanity. Two good people
survived the flood, however. Their names were Pyrrha and
Deucalion, and they lived by hiding in a chest. The chest
floated to the one place on earth that wasn't under water—the
peak of Mount Parnassus. Zeus felt sorry for the two, and so
he drained away the floodwaters. Pyrrha and Deucalion then
were told to scatter stones across the land. The stones turned
into people, and the human race continued.

The rainbow seen by Noah and his family after surviving the flood

To Jewish and Christian people, the best-known flood story is the one about Noah and his ark. You can read about Noah in the book of the Bible called *Genesis.* According to this story, God became very upset when He saw how wicked people had become. He decided to destroy everyone except a good man named Noah and his family. God told Noah to build a great boat, an ark. Noah gathered his family in the ark. He also gathered at least two of each kind of animal in the ark. It rained for forty days and forty nights, but Noah, his family, and the animals survived the flood. They left the ark and began to repopulate the planet. God said that He would never send another flood to destroy mankind. As a symbol of that promise, God put a rainbow up in the sky.

The Indians had many interesting flood stories. The Sherente Indians of Brazil said that long ago the gods were angry because people were fighting too much. One god took the shape of a man. He had sores all over his body and was very ugly. As he went from town to town, people were cruel to him. One man alone welcomed him into his house. The god told this man to catch a pigeon. After the man shot a pigeon with an arrow, the bird turned into a boat. Rain began to fall, causing a vast flood. All the people drowned except this good man and his family, who climbed into the boat.

The Miwok Indians of California said that long ago the animals knew that a flood was coming. They survived by going to the top of the highest mountain. Human beings, however, were drowned. Eagle, Coyote, and the other animals were lonely without people. In a dream, a skeleton told Coyote that Coyote could make people come back if he sang. Coyote sang for days and days. Finally, an old man appeared, followed by more people. According to this story, the coyote sings today because he is so happy that he brought the people back.

The Indians of North America built mounds. Some of the mounds were used as places of refuge during times of flood. The ancient Chinese built dikes to restrain the Yellow River from flooding. But ancient people could do very little to prevent or predict floods. This was because they had little understanding of the causes of floods.

What Floods Are and Why They Occur

A flood is an overflow of water onto what is usually dry land. Water covers about three-quarters of the earth's surface. It is natural for some of it to flood the land from time to time.

When they read the word *flood,* many people picture only river floods. Ocean water can flood the land, too. The causes of river floods and seacoast floods are quite different. They both have the same result, however—water flows onto what is usually dry land.

Causes of River Floods

Rainstorms are a major cause of river floods. Rivers are almost always lower than the surrounding land. During heavy rainstorms, large quantities of water run down into the rivers. The rivers rise higher and higher. If more water reaches a river than its bed can hold, a flood occurs.

In June of 1972, the Susquehanna River raged through the downtown business section of Wilkes-Barre, Pennsylvania, causing millions of dollars of damage. At center, smoke rises from a burning building as fire fighters train hoses on the blaze.

*Heavy winter snows (above) melt
each spring and sometimes cause
rivers to flood. Dams (right)
help keep some rivers from flooding.*

Each spring, melting snow turns into water. If enough of
this water trickles down into the rivers, floods result.

In many parts of the world, dams help keep rivers from
flooding. They block off water and store it in large lakes.
Occasionally a dam breaks. When that happens, an entire lake
of water can be dumped onto dry land. Some of the worst
floods in America's history have been caused by burst dams.

Causes of Seacoast Floods

Have you ever moved your legs in the bathtub and
observed the waves that are created? Movements of the
ground, called *earthquakes,* sometimes occur beneath the
oceans. The shaking ground sets off waves, called *tsunamis.*
Tsunamis travel long distances across the ocean before

This sixteen-foot storm surge created by Hurricane Eloise in 1975 smashed into the northwest Florida coast.

striking land. Coasts are flooded, people drown, and buildings are smashed.

In 1896 an earthquake off the coast of Japan created a tsunami that was 110 feet high when it struck the beach at Sanriku, Japan. About 27,000 people were killed in that city.

Eruptions of volcanoes also can create tsunami waves. In 1883 an eruption of the volcano Krakatoa created tsunamis that drowned 37,000 people.

Hurricanes (called *typhoons* or *cyclones* in other parts of the world) have caused some of our planet's deadliest floods. The two-hundred-mile-per-hour winds of these storms whip up huge ocean waves. These waves, known collectively as a *storm surge,* flood the seacoast. A storm surge from a hurricane was the big killer in the United States' worst natural disaster — the Galveston hurricane of 1900. Sea storms less intense than hurricanes also can cause flooding of coastal regions.

31

The power of the 1964 tsunami in Alaska caused this damage in Seward (above) and drove a plank through a truck tire at Whittier (right).

The Power of Water

We bathe and swim in water. We drink it. About two-thirds of the human body consists of water. You may find it difficult to picture this familiar substance tearing whole cities apart and drowning thousands of people. Yet water has done that many times.

Part of water's power comes from its weight. Water is surprisingly heavy. One cubic foot of water weighs about 62.4 pounds. During Colorado's 1976 Big Thompson flood, about forty thousand cubic feet of water passed through the Narrows of the canyon each second. If you want to know how many pounds of water flowed through the Narrows per second, multiply the numbers.

Another part of water's power comes from its ability to travel fast. During flash floods, river water may move at twenty miles per hour or more. Tsunamis can travel at speeds of *six hundred* miles per hour.

If you've ever been knocked down by a wave at the beach, you have some idea of the power behind water's weight and rapid movement. Such a wave is harmless compared to a tsunami or a flash flood in a canyon.

32

4/SOME FAMOUS FLOODS

Regardless of the cause, floods kill in two main ways. Some people are drowned. Others are battered to death in the mess of houses, trees, and vehicles that gets swept along by the water. Here are the stories of some of the world's most famous floods.

Seacoast Flood from a Volcano - Krakatoa, 1883

In 1883 a volcano named Krakatoa erupted. The explosion was one of the most violent ever known to man. Picture an island blowing most of itself right off the surface of our planet. Imagine pieces of that island soaring fifty miles into the sky, then circling the earth for months. Think of a noise so loud that it awoke people in Australia, two thousand miles away. If you can imagine all that, you have some idea of the power of this eruption.

Though Krakatoa erupted again in 1927 (below), that eruption did not create the same kind of giant tsunami waves that caused thousands of deaths in 1883.

Although no one lived on Krakatoa, the eruption caused many thousands of deaths. Giant tsunami waves were created. These waves rushed across the sea at more than three hundred miles per hour. When they neared shore, they piled up into walls of water five stories high. People were drowned and villages destroyed on the islands of Java and Sumatra. In all, about 37,000 people perished, making this the worst tsunami disaster in history.

The Deadliest Flood Ever - China's Yellow River, 1887

China—the country with the most people in the world—has had some of the worst natural disasters. Many times the country has been shaken by earthquakes, lashed by typhoons, and flooded by rivers. Some of China's worst floods have occurred where the country's civilization was born: along the Yellow River.

The river received its name because of the yellow earth carried by its waters. So much of this sediment has been deposited on the riverbed that in some places the river is actually higher than the surrounding land. In those places the Chinese for centuries have built and maintained *levees,* or walls, to keep the water from flooding the land. But since ancient times, Yellow River floods have occurred despite all efforts. Some of the floods have even caused the river to change its course.

In the fall of 1887, Honan Province in eastern China was pelted by heavy rains. The Yellow River rose higher and higher. Finally it burst through seventy-foot-tall levees. The water flooded eleven cities and hundreds of smaller villages. At least 900,000 people drowned. This was the deadliest flood

Some of China's worst floods have occurred along the Yellow River, even though levees and dams are used for flood control.
Top left: So much sediment has been deposited at Kaifeng that the riverbed here is several feet higher than the surrounding countryside.
Left: The water being discharged through the Sanmenhsia sluice gates contains so much sediment that it almost looks like chocolate milk.
Below: The Yellow River and levee at Zengzhou.

The South Fork Dam near Johnstown, Pennsylvania (above) was built in 1851 to hold back the waters of the Little Conemaugh River. But by 1889, the dam was in very poor condition.

that has ever occurred. It was also one of the deadliest natural disasters of any kind ever to strike human beings.

Thousands of square miles of farm crops were covered by water. In places, the water stood twenty feet deep above the farms. It took two years to subside. With crops ruined, many people had nothing to eat. Exactly how many thousands died of hunger is not known.

In 1939, there were more terrible floods of the Yellow and other rivers in northern China. This time, at least half a million people drowned. It is thought that several million more died of hunger following these floods.

Burst Dam - The Johnstown Flood, 1889

In 1889 Johnstown, Pennsylvania was a steel-making city of thirty thousand people. Fourteen miles from Johnstown, a dam held back the waters of the Little Conemaugh River. The body of water behind the dam was Lake Conemaugh. Between Lake Conemaugh and Johnstown, the land sloped downhill.

By 1889 the dam was known to be in poor condition. Whenever it rained hard, the people of Johnstown worried that the lake would burst through the dam and tumble down into their city. A country club owned the dam. Its members sailed and fished in the lake. But the country club did little to keep the dam in good condition.

May 30, 1889 was Memorial Day. Civil War veterans marched in the Johnstown parade. After the celebrations ended, it began to rain. The rain came down hard and steady. In places, almost a foot of water fell in a few hours.

On the morning of May 31, the waters of the Little Conemaugh River and Lake Conemaugh rose rapidly. By eleven-thirty in the morning, the lake's waters reached almost to the top of the dam. Shortly after that, the waters spilled over the top. Then at about three in the afternoon, the entire dam collapsed. "It seemed to push out all at once," said a boy who witnessed the disaster. Roaring like a gigantic waterfall, a thirty-foot-tall wall of water began its downhill rush toward Johnstown. Within thirty-six minutes, the entire lake had drained and was heading toward the city.

Before the flood reached Johnstown, it smashed through the towns of Mineral Point, East Conemaugh, and Woodvale. At Mineral Point, every house was washed away. At East Conemaugh, 50 passengers from a train had to run for their lives as the wave approached. At least 20 of them died in the water. Survivors from the train later said that the wall of water at that point was fifty feet high. At Woodvale—just one mile from Johnstown—314 people were killed and every building but one was destroyed.

At three o'clock on the afternoon of May 31, 1889, the dam collapsed. A monstrous wall of water roared down the valley toward Johnstown, picking up trains, people, trees, houses, and everything else in its path.

The people of Johnstown heard a low rumble that grew into a thunderous roar. Looking to the east they saw a monstrous wave carrying trains, people, trees, and other debris toward them at sixty miles per hour. There was nothing they could do. Johnstown was smashed in ten minutes. People died by the hundreds.

The floodwaters were stopped by a huge bridge in Johnstown. Houses and other debris piled up against the bridge. About two thousand persons who had survived the flood were trapped in these houses. Probably because stoves were overturned, the buildings caught fire. Hundreds who had escaped drowning died in the flames.

On the morning of June 1, more than 2,200 people lay dead in and around Johnstown. Years later, the bodies of flood victims were still being found.

Between 1937 and 1943, river walls and other flood-control projects were built for Johnstown. But because the city lies in a valley alongside the Conemaugh and Little Conemaugh rivers, Johnstown is still vulnerable to floods. When the Conemaugh River flooded again in 1977, eighty-five people died in Johnstown.

The flood
caused extremely
heavy damage
in this area of
Johnstown.

The Masonic
Relief set up
this commissary
at Bedford and
Baumer streets
to help
survivors.

Those who lost
their homes
built temporary
shelters on
the hillside.
Men occupied
one area and
women another.

The Mississippi River Flood · 1927

The Indians called the river *Mississippi* meaning "Father of Waters." The Mississippi is the longest river in the United States. Farmers have long grown cotton and other crops in the river's fertile valleys. For hundreds of years, the river has served as a water highway down the middle of the country. Some of the major cities in the United States grew up on the banks of the Mississippi. Minneapolis, St. Louis, Memphis, and New Orleans are just four of them.

Those who settled along the river sometimes saw their towns and farms destroyed by floods. They tried to do something about it. Starting in the 1700s, levees were built along the river. The levees, made of piled-up dirt and sandbags, helped keep the river from overflowing. But no matter how big, strong, or numerous the levees were, the Mississippi continued to flood from time to time.

In late 1926, torrential rains fell over the central United States. Such rivers as the Wabash, Tennessee, Cumberland, and Illinois rose. These rivers, which flow into the Mississippi, raised the level of the Father of Waters.

On Easter Sunday, 1912, residents of Greenville, Mississippi walked along the Mississippi River levee during high water.

When the levee broke in 1927, the waters of the Mississippi flooded Greenville.

More heavy rainstorms in the spring of 1927 made things worse. In April it looked as though the river would burst through the levees in several places. Workers piled up more sandbags and dirt to strengthen the levees. On April 21 a man working on the levee at Mound Landing, Mississippi reported by phone: "We can't hold it much longer!" Soon after that he cried, "There she goes!" The collapsing levee sent many workers to their deaths and unleashed a torrent of water. This marked the beginning of one of the country's worst floods.

During the next several weeks, the Mississippi broke more levees and splashed over the tops of others. Eventually, more than sixteen million acres of land in seven states were under water. In some areas, only Indian mounds, tall trees, and telephone poles could be seen above the water.

Because the waters moved at only fourteen miles a day, most people had time to reach higher ground. Some who waited too long had to climb onto bridges or rooftops. There they waited to be rescued by boat or seaplane. Hundreds of boat owners volunteered in the rescue work.

It is estimated that between 250 and 500 persons died in

this flood. More than 160,000 homes were flooded, leaving half a million people homeless. In addition, millions of farm animals were drowned, and many crops were washed away.

In the late 1930s the United States government began a major flood-control program for the Mississippi River. Stronger levees were built. Dams were built to keep other rivers from flooding the Mississippi. Large channels, called *floodways,* were constructed to hold future floodwaters. These efforts have helped. The Mississippi has had other floods, but none has been as deadly as the one of 1927.

Sea Flood from an Earthquake - The Hawaiian Tsunamis, 1946

At two o'clock on the morning of April 1, 1946, an earthquake rocked the Aleutian Islands, in Alaska. As huge blocks of rock broke beneath the ocean, tsunamis were born. The waves zoomed across the ocean at five hundred miles per hour. Hour after hour the waves continued on their deadly course. In the middle of the ocean they were barely noticeable. But when the waves approached land, they piled up into huge walls of water.

At about seven o'clock in the morning, the tsunamis smashed into the Hawaiian Islands, 2,400 miles from where the quake had occurred. People near the coast saw fifty-foot waves hit the beaches. About 170 persons drowned in the titanic waves. Hundreds of buildings were destroyed.

After this disaster, the United States set up the Pacific Tsunami Warning System to warn people of approaching sea waves. Later you will learn how it warns people of seacoast floods.

Though Hawaiians ran from the giant tsunamis of 1946, about 170 persons drowned.

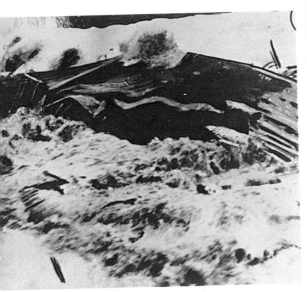

These fifty-foot tsunami waves hit Hawaii's beaches on April 1, 1946.

The Netherlands' Sea Flood, 1953

The term *sea level* refers to the level of our planet's oceans. Most of the land on earth lies above sea level. But there is a European country in which two-fifths of the land lies below sea level. That country is The Netherlands.

When people first settled in The Netherlands, they found that the sea often flooded the coast. About two thousand years ago, the people began their long fight against the sea. They piled up mounds of dirt and stones to keep out the sea. These first barriers didn't do the job very well. Floods in the years 1287 and 1421 took many thousands of lives. But gradually the people of The Netherlands, called the Dutch, learned to build strong *seawalls,* or *dikes.* With the sea held back, cities and farms were built along the coast. By the year 1600 the Dutch had a line of strong dikes to protect their country from the sea.

The Dutch kept their dikes in good condition. They knew that if a dike broke, their country could suffer a terrible flooding. The Dutch also knew that they never could be completely safe from the sea. An unusually strong storm could break dikes and send the sea rolling into the country. That was what happened on January 31, 1953.

The storm came at a particularly bad time. The sun and the moon cause the level of the oceans to rise and fall. These changes in water level are called *tides*. When the storm struck The Netherlands on that last day of January, the tide was unusually high. So the waters of the North Sea were higher than usual against the dikes. The storm winds made things worse. They whipped up huge waves on the North Sea. The waves smashed against the dikes in the southwest part of the country. Waves splashed over the tops of some dikes and smashed holes right through others. Soon the waters of the North Sea were rushing into The Netherlands.

About two thousand people died in this flood. People had to climb up into their attics and onto rooftops to survive. Some drifted along on pieces of wood or furniture until they were rescued by boat. The United States and other countries loaned helicopters to The Netherlands to aid in the rescues.

This dike near Terneuzen broke during the storms that hit The Netherlands in February, 1953.

Waters from the North Sea flooded the ancient Dutch town of Nieuwerkerk during the 1953 tragedy.

After this flood, the Dutch built stronger dikes and new dams. They hope that these efforts will keep their country safe from floods like the one of 1953.

The Worst Sea Flood Ever - The East Pakistan Cyclone, 1970

The deadliest hurricane to strike the United States was the one that hit Galveston, Texas in 1900. At least 7,200 people died in that disaster, mostly by drowning. It was the worst natural disaster of any kind in the nation's history.

In the Bay of Bengal, the storms that we call hurricanes are called cyclones. The countries that lie along the Bay of Bengal have experienced far deadlier storms than the Galveston hurricane. In 1876 a cyclone that slammed into India drowned 200,000 persons. An even deadlier cyclone struck East Pakistan, now the country of Bangladesh, in 1970.

A Pakistani man sobs on the shoulders of a friend after losing his entire family in the tidal wave created by the 1970 cyclone.

The people of East Pakistan had little warning that the cyclone was coming. Most of them were asleep when the storm whirled onto the coast from the Bay of Bengal. By the time the people were awakened by the roar, it was too late. Leaving their huts, they saw a twenty-five-foot-high wall of water rushing toward them. The cyclone's 120-mile-per-hour winds had driven Bay of Bengal waters onto the coast.

Thousands of people were drowned immediately. Luckier ones climbed trees or grabbed the tails of swimming cattle. One young man, Modan Modan Shaha, held onto a bamboo pole for five hours to keep from drowning. You remember the Greek myth about the two people who survived a flood by floating inside a wooden chest. In one town a man stuffed his six grandchildren into a wooden chest. When they reached shore three days later, the children were safe.

There were few survival stories in this flood, however. When the waters went down, thousands of bodies could be seen lying in the muck. In some towns not one person was left alive.

The exact number of people who died in this sea flood is not known. Almost certainly the number topped 500,000. It was the deadliest storm and the worst seacoast flood of all time.

SOME FAMOUS RIVER FLOODS

Date	River	Country	Estimated Deaths
1824	Neva River	Russia	10,000
1861	Sacramento River	California, U.S.A.	700
1874	Several rivers	Western Pennsylvania, U.S.A.	220
1887	Yellow River	China	At least 900,000, possibly many more
1911	Yangtze River	China	100,000
March 25-27, 1913	Miami River and Ohio River	Ohio and Indiana, U.S.A.	732
Spring, 1927	Mississippi River	U.S.A.	In the hundreds
1931	Yangtze River	China	145,000
1939	All rivers in the northern part of the country	China	At least 500,000, possibly many more
August, 1954	Flash flood in a gully	Iran	2,000
Summer, 1955	River systems near the mouths of the Ganges River	East Pakistan (now Bangladesh) and India	2,000
November 4-5, 1966	Arno, Po, and Adige rivers	Italy	At least 113
May-June 1970	Danube River	Romania	215
July, 1970	Alaknanda River	India	600
November, 1970	Magdalena River	Colombia	In the hundreds
July 31-August 1, 1976	Flash flood of the Big Thompson River	Colorado, U.S.A.	139
1981	Yangtze River	China	At least 3,000

Johnstown, Pennsylvania during a 1977 flood

SOME FAMOUS FLOODS ASSOCIATED WITH DAM FAILURES

Date	Dam	Country	Estimated Deaths
May 16, 1874	Dam on Mill Creek	Western Massachusetts, U.S.A.	144
May 31, 1889	South Fork Dam	Johnstown, Pennsylvania, U.S.A.	More than 2,200
March 13, 1928	Saint Francis Dam	Santa Paula, California, U.S.A.	450
January 9, 1959	Dam on Tera River	Vega de Tera, Spain	135
December 2, 1959	Malpasset Dam	Fréjus, France	412
October 9, 1963	Vaiont Dam	Italy	At least 2,000
September 4, 1967	Kolya Dam (collapse caused by an earthquake)	India	More than 200
February 26, 1972	Coal-waste dam on Buffalo Creek	West Virginia, U.S.A.	125
June 9-10, 1972	Canyon Lake Dam	Rapid City, South Dakota, U.S.A.	242

Rescue operations during a July, 1975 flash flood

SOME FAMOUS SEACOAST FLOODS

Date	Cause of Flood	Places Hardest Hit	Estimated Deaths (for hurricanes and other storms, this includes deaths from wind, which usually causes only about 10% of the fatalities)
December 14, 1287	Sea storm	The Netherlands	50,000
November 26-27, 1703	Hurricane	England	8,000
November 1, 1755	Tsunamis created by an earthquake in Portgual	Portugal and Morocco	At least 10,000
October 31, 1876	Cyclone	Bakarganj, India	200,000
October 8, 1881	Typhoon	Indochina	300,000
June 5, 1882	Cyclone	Bombay, India	100,000
August 27, 1883	Tsunamis created by the eruption of Krakatoa volcano	Java and Sumatra	37,000
June 15, 1896	Tsunamis created by an underwater earthquake	Sanriku, Japan	27,000
August 27-September 15, 1900	Hurricane	Galveston, Texas	At least 7,200
September 6-20, 1928	Hurricane	Southern Florida	Approximately 2,000
September 10-22, 1938	Hurricane	Long Island and southern New England, U.S.A.	Approximately 600
October 16, 1942	Cyclone	Bengal, India	40,000
April 1, 1946	Tsunamis created by an earthquake in Alaska	Hawaii	173
January 31, 1953	Sea storm	The Netherlands	Approximately 2,000
May 22, 1960	Tsunamis created by an earthquake in Chile	Hawaii, Japan, Philippines, New Zealand	In the hundreds
May 28-29, 1963	Cyclone	East Pakistan (now Bangladesh)	22,000
November 12-13, 1970	Cyclone	East Pakistan (now Bangladesh)	At least 500,000 (the most ever killed by any kind of storm)
November 19, 1977	Cyclone	India	15,000

Levees, dikes, dams, floodways, and spillways are used all over the world to help prevent river floods. During the floods of 1982, thirty thousand volunteers, mostly teenagers, filled thousands of sandbags and stacked them on the Fort Wayne, Indiana dikes.

5/PROTECTING PEOPLE FROM FLOODS

Each year thousands of people die in floods. A 1977 seacoast flood created by a cyclone killed fifteen thousand people in India. A 1981 river flood in China killed at least three thousand. If you read the newspaper or watch the news on television, you will find that every year there are major floods in many parts of the world.

The United States has not experienced floods as deadly as those that have occurred in China, Bangladesh, and other countries. Nonetheless, floods are the most serious of all natural disasters to strike America. During the past thirty years, flash floods of rivers have killed about four thousand Americans. During that same period, about fifteen thousand Americans drowned in floods caused by hurricanes.

Preventing Floods

Long before the birth of Christ, the Chinese built levees to prevent rivers from flooding. Today levees are still the main flood-control method in China. Dams are also an important part of China's flood-control system. The dams stop the flow of water on the rivers. Behind the dams, the water is stored in *reservoirs*. When the Yellow River is flooding, some of the water is diverted into what are called *holding basins*. After the flood, the water is pumped out of these basins.

In the United States, the first levees were built in 1718 to keep the Mississippi River from flooding. Today the United States has thousands of miles of levees on the Mississippi and other rivers. The levees are made of concrete, piled-up dirt, and sandbags. When the rivers rise higher than their natural banks, the levees help prevent floods. As in China, dams and reservoirs are important to the flood-control system in the United States. In addition, many floodways, which are somewhat like China's holding basins, have been built. Instead of merely holding the extra water, however, the floodways take it to the sea. The United States also has seawalls to help protect coastal cities from hurricane storm surges.

In most countries that have experienced floods, people have made efforts to prevent future disasters. The Netherlands has dikes to protect the country from the North Sea. France, England, Germany, Russia, and Italy have built levees to prevent river floods. Russia and India have large numbers of dams and reservoirs for flood-control purposes.

Predicting Floods

No matter what precautions are taken, floods will occur from time to time. The best way to keep people safe from floods is to get them out of the area before the floods occur. To do that, scientists must be able to predict floods.

In the United States, the National Weather Service has the job of predicting the country's weather. Part of this job includes predicting conditions that may create floods. The National Weather Service operates hundreds of weather offices throughout the country. The agency also operates special offices to predict river floods, floods from hurricanes, and floods from tsunamis.

Meteorologists (weather scientists) who work for the National Weather Service have many tools to help them make

The Morganza Spillway (above) diverted water from the Mississippi River on the right to the Atchafalaya Floodway on the left during the 1973 floods.

their flood predictions. *Weather satellities* and *radar* are two of the main ones. High above the earth, the satellites take pictures of our planet's cloud patterns. These pictures help meteorologists see where rainstorms, hurricanes, and other storms are likely to occur. Radar shows places where rain or snow is actually falling. *Weather balloons,* ships at sea, and observers on the ground provide additional information for the Weather Service.

Predicting River Floods

In 1973 there was a big flood of the Mississippi River. The property damage came to more than $150 million. Very few lives were lost, however. The experts had predicted that a flood was coming. People fled their homes before it occurred.

As these pictures prove, floodwaters do great damage to vehicles, farms, buildings, city streets, and anything else in their path.

The pictures on this page show the widespread damage that occurred during the Johnstown Flood of 1977.

The National Weather Service operates thirteen River Forecast Centers in the United States. The scientists at these centers watch for conditions that may create floods.

Four factors are important in predicting a river flood. How much water can the riverbed hold? How high is the river? How much moisture is expected in the near future? How much of that moisture will reach the river?

The river specialists make measurements so that they will know how much water the riverbed can hold. Instruments called *river gauges* help the scientists keep track of the river's height. Experts study the land around the river to determine how much water will reach the river from melting snows or a rainstorm. They study rainfall reports to determine how much water is dropping from the sky. The experts also study radar and satellite reports so that they can figure how much water is expected in the near future. When the scientists think that a flood is going to occur, people are warned.

Many observers use small rain gauges like this one to record rainfall for the National Weather Service flash-flood program.

The flash flood is the most difficult type of river flood to predict. Flash floods come suddenly, after rainstorms or snow melts, usually in mountainous areas. The United States has a special alarm system to warn communities of flash floods. Devices called *flash-flood alarms* have been attached to many bridge piers in rivers. If a river reaches a certain height, the flash-flood alarm sets off a signal that is sent to the town's fire or police station. Sirens are then sounded to warn the people in the area. The flash-flood alarm system is now in operation in about a hundred United States cities and towns.

Predicting Hurricanes

In September of 1979, Hurricane Frederic struck the coast of the southeastern United States. Winds of 145 miles per hour were measured. A ten-foot storm surge flooded the

This staff gauge located on a bridge pier in Maryland is used to measure the depth of the water flowing under the bridge. On the same pier is a flash-flood alert (the small white sensor on the right side of the pier).

*Because the National Hurricane Center tracked Hurricane Frederic before
it slammed into the Gulf Coast of the United States in 1979 (above), people
were warned in time to leave the threatened areas and many lives were saved.*

coast. The water from this surge could have drowned
thousands. But because the people along the coast had been
warned, few people stayed in the dangerous areas. Thanks to
these warnings, only fifteen persons died.

The National Hurricane Center in Miami, Florida forecasts
hurricanes for the United States. As they study the satellite
pictures, the hurricane experts can easily spot the giant
storms long before they strike our coasts. Reports from radar,
weather balloons, and ships at sea also help the hurricane
experts. The scientists don't just study reports. Some of them
make airplane flights right into hurricanes. There they gather
more information for the Hurricane Center.

Many hours before a hurricane slams into the coast, the
scientists have determined its power and movement. They
have a good idea of the size of the storm surge that will
accompany the hurricane. People along the coast then are
warned to leave their homes or to take other action.

The Pacific Tsunami Warning System, headquartered near Honolulu,
Hawaii (above right), was set up after the disastrous tsunami
waves hit Hawaii in 1946. The water wave from that tsunami is shown
as it filled the Wailuka River on Hawaii Island (above left).

Predicting Tsunamis

In 1960 the South American country of Chile was jolted by
a monstrous earthquake. The quake sent tsunamis zooming
across the ocean at four hundred miles per hour.

Scientists of the Pacific Tsunami Warning System,
headquartered near Honolulu, Hawaii, detected these waves.
Twelve hours before the waves reached Hawaii, the people of
that state were warned to get away from the beaches. Most of
them listened. After a journey of seven thousand miles, three
waves struck Hawaii. One was thirty-five feet high. Houses
and hotels were smashed to pieces. Sixty-one persons—many
of whom had ignored the warnings—were killed. Without the
warnings, hundreds might have died.

The Pacific Tsunami Warning System consists of more than
sixty wave-watching stations in the Pacific Ocean. At these
stations, instruments measure slight changes in the ocean.

Seismographs (above) are part of the Pacific Tsunami Warning System. Right: Technicians install a tide gauge at a Pacific Tsunami Warning System tide station.

Instruments called *seismographs* also are part of the warning system. They measure earthquakes that may create tsunamis.

People in Hawaii and along the Pacific coast of the United States are warned when a tsunami takes aim at them. People in Russia, Japan, Mexico, Canada, Chile, Peru, Colombia, New Zealand, and many other nations also are warned of approaching tsunamis.

Protecting Yourself From Floods

Warnings save lives only if people heed them. During floods there are always some people who refuse to leave their homes.

When the National Weather Service thinks that a river, hurricane, or tsunami flood is about to occur, the information is sent to local officials, newspapers, and television and radio stations. Local officials sometimes go door-to-door to tell people of the danger. The important thing to remember is that if you're advised to leave your home—GO! Although the ocean or river may look peaceful, experts may have spotted a hurricane or a rainstorm that will soon cause a flood. Listen to the experts and do what they advise.

Usually there is plenty of time to get out of the way of a hurricane or a flood of a major river. Flash floods, however, don't give much warning time. The National Weather Service gives this advice to protect people from flash floods:

- Avoid camping on low ground right next to rivers or streams.
- Whenever you're near a river, figure out where the high ground is in case you need it.
- If you're in your car and water is rising around it, leave the vehicle and go on foot to higher land. Many people have died in cars that floated away.
- In towns, stay away from sewers or open ditches.
- Always stay away from flooded areas. Some people go into flooded areas to look at the damage. Others return to get valuables from their homes. Some people even canoe or swim into flooded areas. More rain may bring more flooding that can catch such people by surprise.

"Floods are the most destructive natural phenomenon we have," says Dr. Robert A. Clark, chief *hydrologist* (water scientist) for the National Weather Service. "But today people are provided with warnings that we didn't have thirty-five years ago.

"Today we have satellites and radar to help scientists make predictions. We have thousands of automated river gauges and rain gauges. We also have a good communications system to get warnings to people.

"During periods of heavy rain or an approaching hurricane, people should stay tuned to their local radio or television stations. When people are warned that there may be flooding, they should pay close attention to those warnings and do what the authorities advise.

"Flood deaths never can be eliminated totally. But if people listen to the warnings, needless deaths can be avoided."

Glossary

Cyclone   The name for a hurricane that occurs in the Indian Ocean or the South Pacific Ocean

Dike   A bank of earth, clay, sand, stone, concrete, or other materials constructed to keep the sea from flooding the land

Earthquake   A shaking of the earth believed to be caused by movement of the earth's plates against or away from one another

Flash Flood   A sudden flood for which there is little or no warning, usually caused by heavy rains or snow melts in mountainous areas

Flash-Flood Alarm   A sensor that gives a warning if a river reaches a certain height

Flood   A body of water that overflows and covers land that is normally dry

Floodway   A channel that diverts floodwaters

Holding Basin   A reservoir into which floodwaters are diverted

Hurricane   A huge, powerful windstorm that whirls in a circular motion and covers thousands of square miles; it is much larger than a tornado, but its wind are not as strong

Hydrologist   A scientist who studies the waters of the earth

Hypothermia   A severe loss of body heat

Levee   A bank of earth built along a riverbank to keep a river from flooding the land

Radar   An instrument that can detect and locate distant objects by means of reflected radio waves

Reservoir   An artificial lake created when a dam is built, often used to store floodwaters

River Gauge   An instrument used to measure the height of a river

Sea Level   The average level of the surface of ocean waters

Seawall   A wall or embankment built at a shoreline to protect an area from flooding

Seismograph   An instrument that detects earthquakes

Storm Surge   A great mound of water, topped by battering waves, that moves toward shore during a hurricane

Tide   The regular rise and fall of ocean waters caused by the gravitation, or pull, of the moon and the sun

Tsunami   A huge sea wave, sometimes created by an underwater earthquake

Typhoon   The name for a hurricane that occurs in the North Pacific Ocean

Weather Balloon   A balloon that carries instruments aloft to measure the temperature, moisture, and pressure characteristics in the upper air

Weather Satellite   An instrument that orbits thousands of miles above the earth and takes pictures of cloud formations which are relayed to weather stations on the ground

Photo Credits

About the Author

Dennis Fradin attended Northwestern University on a partial creative writing scholarship and graduated in 1967. He has published stories and articles in such places as *Ingenue, The Saturday Evening Post, Scholastic, Chicago, Oui,* and *National Humane Review.* His previous books include the Young People's Stories of Our States series for Childrens Press and *Bad Luck Tony* for Prentice-Hall. He is married and the father of three children.